❧ About This Book ❧

At last! The perfect coloring book for the birder or naturalist, picturing—with the lifelike precision that is a hallmark of David Sibley's work—seventy-five images of birds in flight and at rest. Common and Latin names and the dimensions and weight of each bird are provided. *The Sibley Birds Coloring Field Journal* allows birding enthusiasts to create their own artist's portfolio, restoring color—whether real or imagined—to wings, crest, beaks.

This edition has a versatile flip-back cover binding design that allows for ease of use and portability, encouraging on-the-go artistry and providing a strong surface for colorists. The book is made with heavy-weight paper and includes a selection of David Sibley's original, previously unpublished paintings for reference, from which the line art for coloring has been derived.

In the back of the book, many drawings of the structure and component parts of birds are featured to familiarize the colorist with bird anatomy.

ALSO BY DAVID ALLEN SIBLEY

The Sibley Field Guide to Birds of Eastern North America, Second Edition (2016)

The Sibley Field Guide to Birds of Western North America, Second Edition (2016)

The Sibley Guide to Birds, Second Edition (2014)

The Sibley Guide to Trees (2009)

Sibley's Birding Basics (2002)

The Sibley Guide to Bird Life and Behavior (2001)

These Are Borzoi Books
Published in New York by Alfred A. Knopf

To learn more about the birds featured in this coloring field journal,
see David Sibley's other definitive books on all the birds found in North America,
which provide extraordinary pictorial detail and comprehensive information.

Drawings by Cecilia Lehar

Adapted from the paintings of,

and with an introduction by,

David Allen Sibley

The SIBLEY BIRDS Coloring Field Journal

ALFRED A. KNOPF   New York   2016

THIS IS A BORZOI BOOK
PUBLISHED BY ALFRED A. KNOPF

www.aaknopf.com

Knopf, Borzoi Books, and the colophon are registered trademarks
of Penguin Random House LLC.

The anatomical bird drawings on pages 68–73 originally
appeared in *Sibley's Birding Basics* by David Allen Sibley,
published by Alfred A. Knopf in 2002.

ISBN: 9781524711078

Jacket art and design by Linda Huang

Manufactured in Mexico
First Edition

FRONTIS: **Black-billed Magpie**
Pica hudsonia
L 19" WS 25" WT 6 OZ

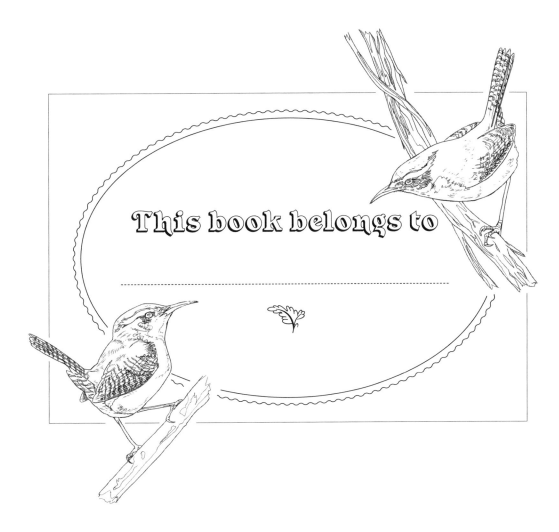

This book belongs to

_____

Contents

Gray-crowned Rosy-Finch

Leucosticte tephrocotis

12

American Goldfinch

Spinus tristis

13

House Sparrow

Passer domesticus

14

Black-capped Chickadee

Poecile atricapilus

14

Dickcissel

Spiza americana

15

Painted Bunting

Passerina ciris

16

Indigo Bunting

Passerina cyanea

17–18

Painted Bunting

Passerina ciris

19

Barn Swallow

Hirundo rustica

20

Cliff Swallow

Petrochelidon pyrrhonota

21

White-winged Crossbill

Loxia leucoptera

22

Green-tailed Towhee

Pipilo chlorurus

23

Mountain Bluebird

Sialia currucoides

24

Eastern Bluebird

Sialia sialis

24

Cedar Waxwing

Bombycilla cedrorum

25

Scarlet Tanager

Piranga olivacea

26

Northern Cardinal

Cardinalis cardinalis

27

Rose-breasted Grosbeak

Pheucticus ludovicianus

28–9

Evening Grosbeak

Coccothraustes vespertinus

30

Yellow-chevroned Parakeet

Brotogeris chiriri

31

Red-winged Blackbird

Agelaius phoeniceus

32

Varied Thrush

Ixoreus naevius

33

Baltimore Oriole

Icterus galbula

34

American Robin

Turdus migratorius

35

Western Meadowlark

Sturnella neglecta

36

Scissor-tailed Flycatcher

Tyrannus forficatus

37

Northern Flicker

Colaptes auratus

38

Belted Kingfisher

Megaceryle alcyon

39

Red-naped Sapsucker

Sphyrapicus nuchalis

40

Red-bellied Woodpecker

Melanerpes carolinensis

41

Lewis's Woodpecker

Melanerpes lewisi

42

Pileated Woodpecker

Dryocopus pileatus

43

Snowy Owl

Bubo scandiacus

44

Northern Saw-whet Owl

Aegolius acadicus

45

Great Horned Owl

Bubo virginianus

46–7

Ring-necked Pheasant

Phasianus colchicus

48

Dusky Grouse

Dendragapus obscurus

49

Gray Partridge

Perdix perdix

50

Sora

Porzana carolina

51

Spectacled Eider

Somateria fischeri

52

Wood Duck

Aix sponsa

53

Yellow-billed Loon

Gavia adamsii

54

Introduction

I don't know why I started drawing birds. I guess a five-year-old doesn't really need a reason. I just liked it. Drawing was a fun way to pass the time, and birds offered a convenient subject for me. My father's ornithology books filled the shelves and offered a fertile supply of shapes, colors, and drama for my imagination.

Over time, as I got more serious about learning the scientific details and drawing realistic birds, drawing became an integral part of my studies. I was approaching birds on two separate tracks—science and art, learning about them and drawing them—and the two were constantly reinforcing each other.

Drawing is, on one level, simply a different way to interact with whatever you are studying. As an artist you face the challenge of trying to translate a living, moving, three-dimensional bird into a few lines on a sheet of paper, and you have to interpret every aspect of its appearance. A vague idea that "the bill is sort of triangular" will not do. You need to know the exact dimensions of that triangle, where it is curved or straight, how

it joins the head, and so on, and that information is conveyed in a picture rather than words. As you work on a sketch you will look at and absorb countless details that a cursory study would miss, details that words could never really capture.

I don't feel like I really know a bird until I've sketched it a few times. This leads to the truism that the most valuable and lasting benefit of sketching is not the physical product (pencil on paper), it is the knowledge and understanding that comes from the process. A drawing is merely the tangible evidence of that understanding.

I may not know why I started drawing birds, but it's easy to say why I still do it. I am enthralled by the exquisite forms and colors of the birds around us, and I get a lot of satisfaction from the simple pleasure of getting to know them. In other words, I just like it.

—David Sibley

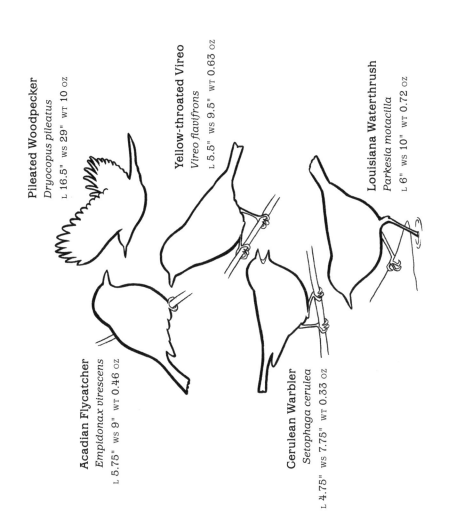

Pileated Woodpecker
Dryocopus pileatus
L 16.5" WS 29" WT 10 OZ

Yellow-throated Vireo
Vireo flavifrons
L 5.5" WS 9.5" WT 0.63 OZ

Louisiana Waterthrush
Parkesia motacilla
L 6" WS 10" WT 0.72 OZ

Acadian Flycatcher
Empidonax virescens
L 5.75" WS 9" WT 0.46 OZ

Cerulean Warbler
Setophaga cerulea
L 4.75" WS 7.75" WT 0.33 OZ

Ruby-throated Hummingbird

Archilochus colubris

L 3.75" WS 4.5" WT 0.11 OZ

Allen's Hummingbird

Selasphorus sasin

L 3.75" WS 4.25" WT 0.11 OZ

Golden-winged Warbler

Vermivora chrysoptera

L 4.75" ws 7.5" wt 0.31 oz

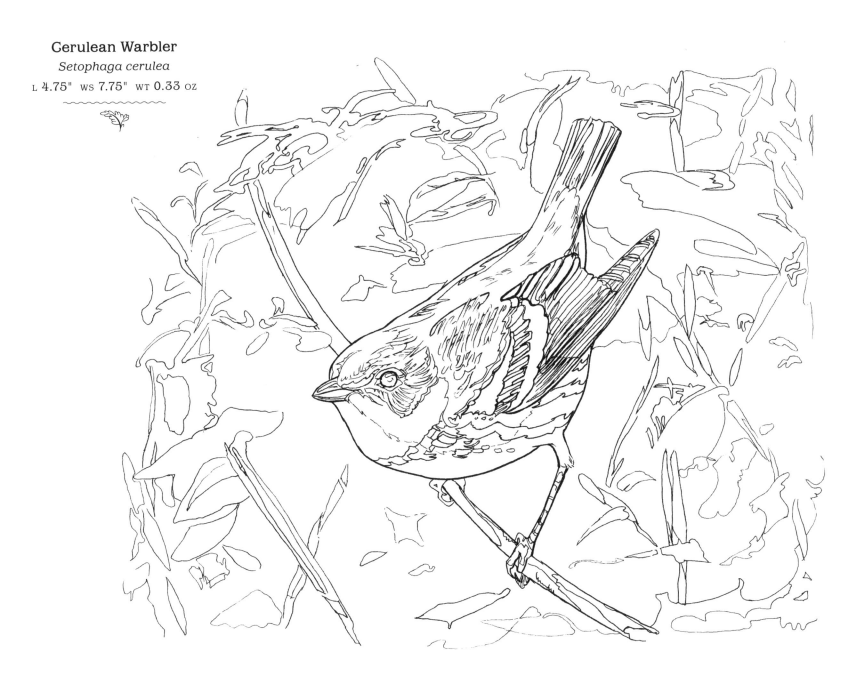

5

Palm Warbler
Setophaga palmarum
L 5.5" WS 8" WT 0.36 OZ

Swainson's Warbler
Limnothlypis swainsonii
L 5.5" WS 9" WT 0.67 OZ

Golden-crowned Kinglet
Regulus satrapa
L 4" WS 7" WT 0.21 OZ

Northern Parula
Setophaga americana
L 4.5" WS 7" WT 0.3 OZ

6

Carolina Wren

Thryothorus ludovicianus

L 5.5" WS 7.5" WT 0.74 OZ

Chestnut-collared Longspur

Calcarius ornatus

L 6" WS 10.5" WT 0.67 OZ

11

Gray-crowned Rosy-Finch
Leucosticte tephrocotis
L 6.25" WS 13" WT 0.91 OZ

American Goldfinch

Spinus tristis

L 5" ws 9" wt 0.46 oz

Black-capped Chickadee

Poecile atricapilus

L 5.25" WS 8" WT 0.39 OZ

House Sparrow

Passer domesticus

L 6.25" WS 9.5" WT 0.98 OZ

Dickcissel
Spiza americana
ʟ 6.25" ᴡꜱ 9.75" ᴡᴛ 0.95 ᴏᴢ

Painted Bunting

Passerina ciris

L 5.5" WS 8.75" WT 0.54 OZ

Indigo Bunting
Passerina cyanea
L 5.5" WS 8" WT 0.51 OZ

17

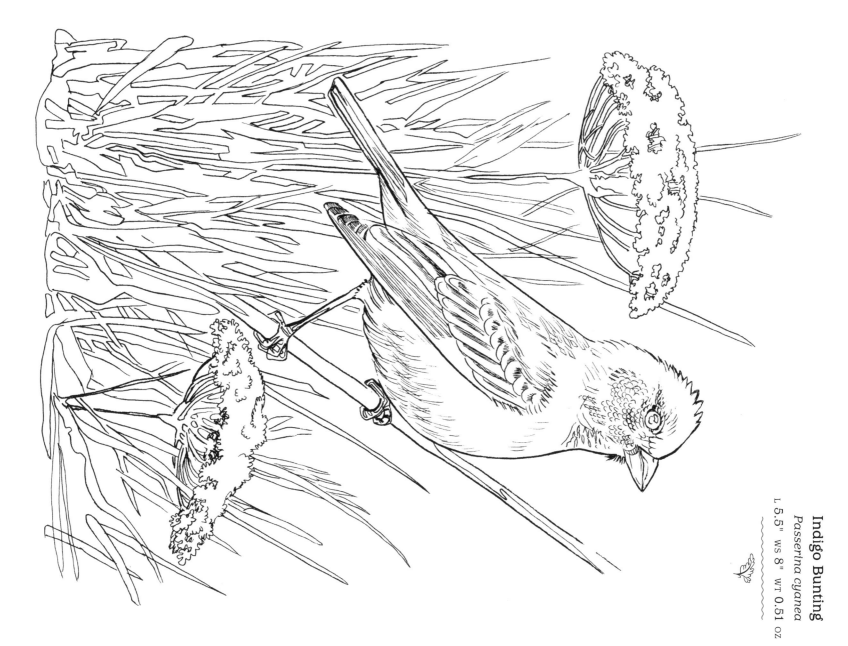

Indigo Bunting
Passerina cyanea
L 5.5" WS 8" WT 0.51 OZ

18

Painted Bunting

Passerina ciris

L 5.5" ws 8.75" wt 0.54 oz

Barn Swallow
Hirundo rustica
L 6.75" WS 15" WT 0.67 OZ

Cliff Swallow
Petrochelidon pyrrhonota
ʟ 5.5" ᴡs 13.5" ᴡᴛ 0.74 oz

White-winged Crossbill

Loxia leucoptera

L 6.5" ws 10.5" wt 0.91 oz

Green-tailed Towhee
Pipilo chlorurus

L 7.25" WS 9.75" WT 1 OZ

23

Mountain Bluebird
Sialia currucoides
L 7.25" WS 14" WT 1 OZ

Eastern Bluebird
Sialia sialis
L 7" WS 13" WT 1.1 OZ

Cedar Waxwing
Bombycilla cedrorum
L 7.25" WS 12" WT 1.1 OZ

Scarlet Tanager
Piranga olivacea
L 7"   WS 11.5"   WT 0.98 OZ

26

Northern Cardinal

Cardinalis cardinalis

L 8.75" WS 12" WT 1.6 OZ

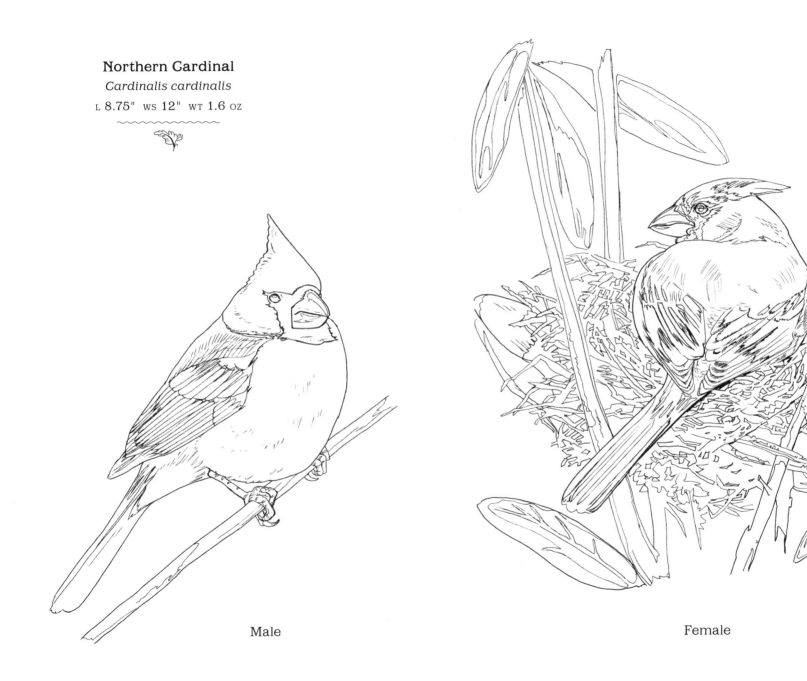

Male

Female

Rose-breasted Grosbeak

Pheucticus ludovicianus

L 8" ws 12.5" wt 1.6 oz

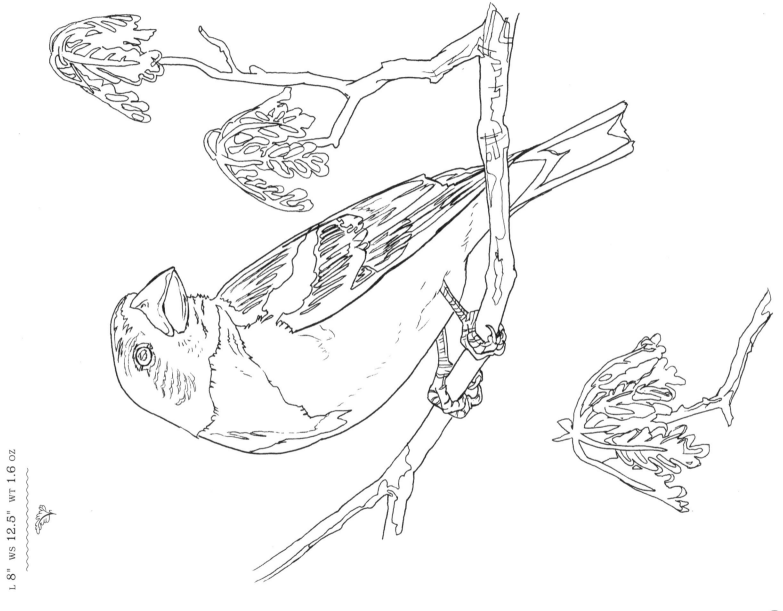

Rose-breasted Grosbeak

Pheucticus ludovicianus

L 8" WS 12.5" WT 1.6 OZ

Evening Grosbeak
Coccothraustes vespertinus
L 8" WS 14" WT 2.1 oz

Yellow-chevroned Parakeet
Brotogeris chiriri
L 8.75" WS 15" WT 2.1 OZ

31

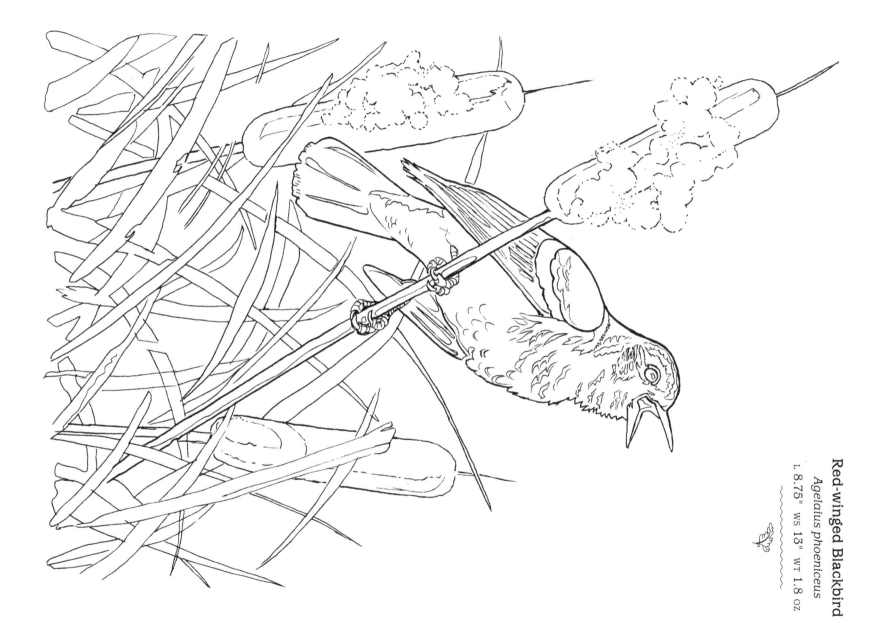

Red-winged Blackbird
Agelaius phoeniceus
L 8.75" WS 13" WT 1.8 OZ

32

33

Baltimore Oriole

Icterus galbula

L 8.75" WS 11.5" WT 1.2 OZ

American Robin

Turdus migratorius

L 10" WS 17" WT 2.7OZ

Scissor-tailed Flycatcher
Tyrannus forficatus
L 10" WS 15" WT 1.5 OZ

37

Northern Flicker

Colaptes auratus

L 12.5" WS 20" WT 4.6 OZ

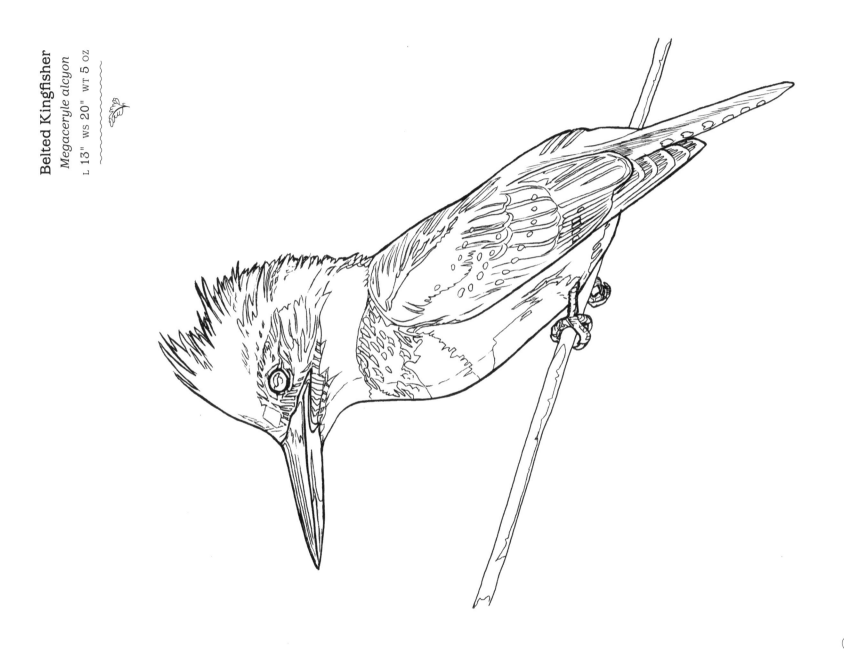

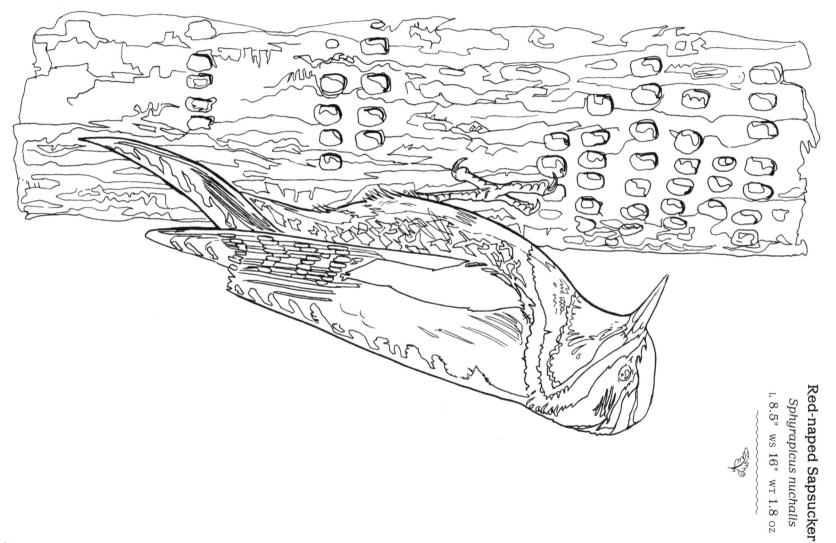

Red-naped Sapsucker
Sphyrapicus nuchalis
L 8.5" WS 16" WT 1.8 OZ

40

Red-bellied Woodpecker

Melanerpes carolinensis

L 9.25" WS 16" WT 2.2 OZ

41

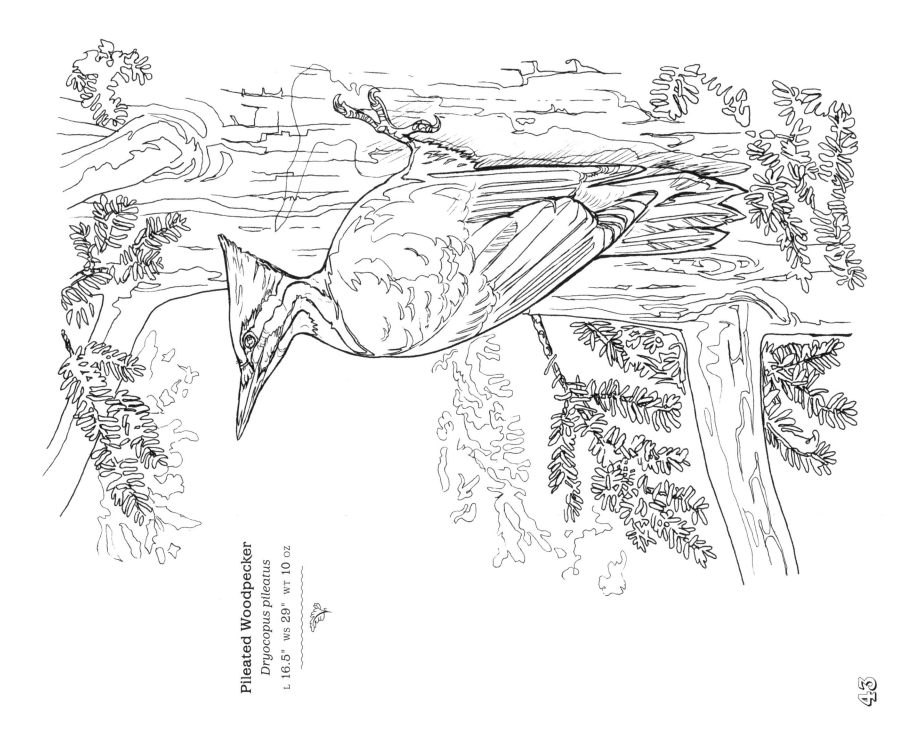

Pileated Woodpecker
Dryocopus pileatus
L 16.5" WS 29" WT 10 OZ

43

Snowy Owl

Bubo scandiacus

L 23" WS 52" WT 4 LB

Northern Saw-whet Owl
Aegolius acadicus
L 8"   ws 17"   wt 2.8 oz

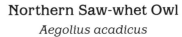

45

Great Horned Owl

Bubo virginianus

L 22" WS 44" WT 3.1 LB

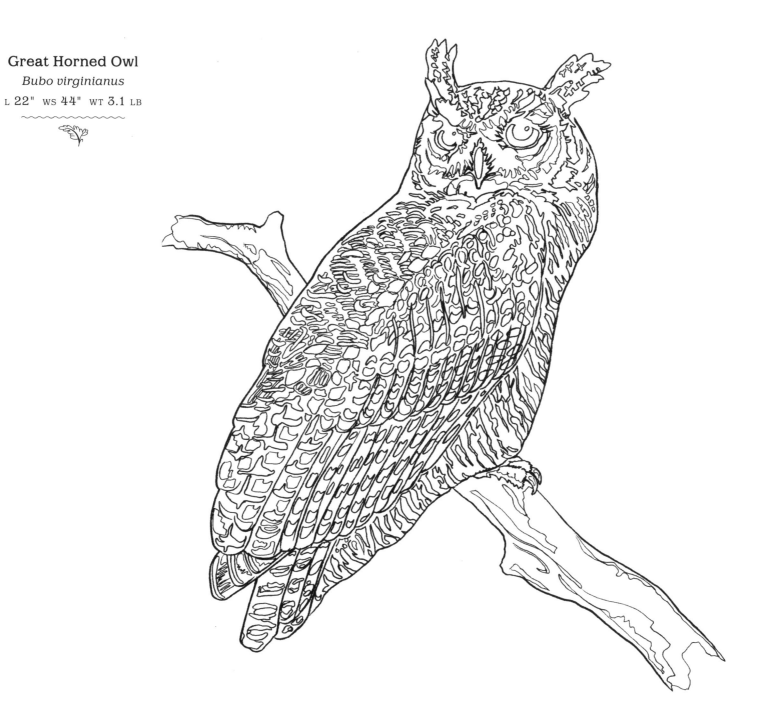

Great Horned Owl
Bubo virginianus
L 22" WS 44" WT 3.1 LB

47

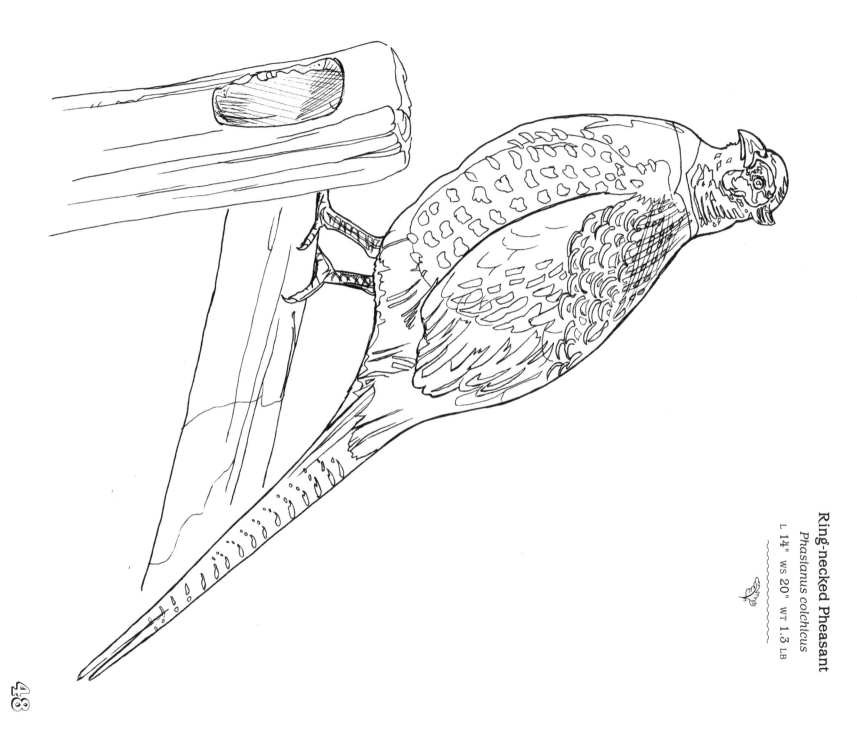

Ring-necked Pheasant

Phasianus colchicus

L 14" WS 20" WT 1.3 LB

48

49

Gray Partridge

Perdix perdix

L 12.5" WS 19" WT 14 OZ

Sora

Porzana carolina

L 8.75" WS 14" WT 2.6 OZ

Spectacled Eider
Somateria fischeri

L 21" ws 33" wt 3.4 lb

Wood Duck

Aix sponsa

L 18.5" WS 30" WT 1.8 LB

53

Yellow-billed Loon
Gavia adamsii

L 35" WS 49" WT 11.8 LB

Roseate Tern
Sternula antillarum
L 12.5" ws 29" wt 3.9 oz

Black-necked Stilt
Himantopus mexicanus
L 14" ws 29" wt 6 oz

Black Rail
Laterallus jamaicensis
L 6" ws 9" wt 1.1 oz

55

Roseate Spoonbill
Platalea ajaja
L 32" WS 50" WT 3.3 LB

56

Blue-footed Booby

Sula nebouxii

L 32" WS 62" WT 3.4 LB

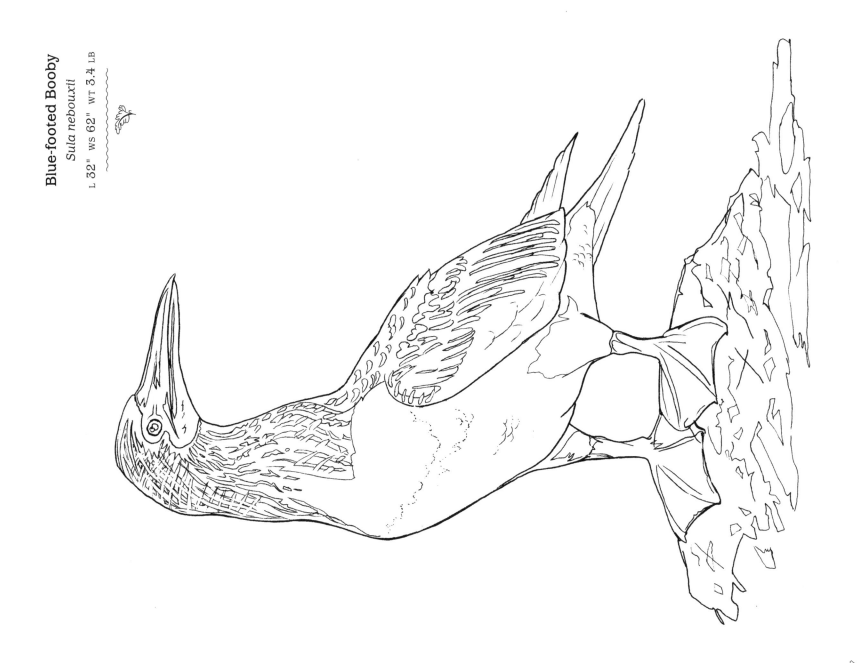

Rock Ptarmigan (chick)
Lagopus muta
Adult: L 14" WS 23" WT 15 oz

Surfbird (chick)
Calidris virgata
Adult: L 10" WS 26" WT 7 oz

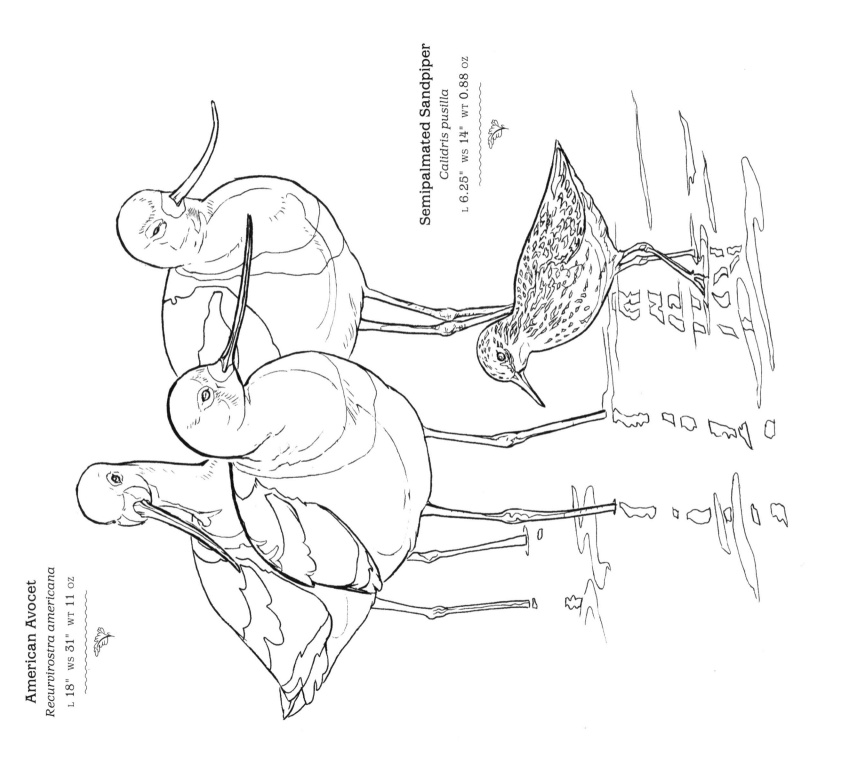

American Avocet

Recurvirostra americana

L 18" WS 31" WT 11 OZ

Semipalmated Sandpiper

Calidris pusilla

L 6.25" WS 14" WT 0.88 OZ

Great Blue Heron
Ardea herodias

L 54" WS 72" WT 6.4 LB

60

Black-necked Stilt

Himantopus mexicanus

L 14" WS 29" WT 6 OZ

Tufted Puffin

Fratercula cirrhata

L 15" WS 25" WT 1.7 LB

62

American Bittern

Botaurus lentiginosus

L 28" WS 42" WT 1.5 LB

Bald Eagle

Haliaeetus leucocephalus

L 31" WS 80" WT 9.5 LB

Merlin

Falco columbarius

L 10" WS 24" WT 6.5 OZ

65

Red-tailed Hawk

Buteo jamaicensis

L 19" WS 49" WT 2.4 LB

Red-tailed Hawk

Buteo jamaicensis

L 19" WS 49" WT 2.4 LB

67

The Anatomy of Birds

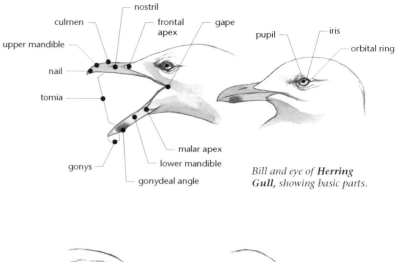

Bill and eye of **Herring Gull,** showing basic parts.

culmen · nostril · frontal apex · gape · pupil · iris · orbital ring · upper mandible · nail · tomia · gonys · malar apex · lower mandible · gonydeal angle

*A **Purple Finch** with representative feathers from different parts of the body. On the left side is a range of feathers from the wings and tail; on the right side three body feathers. Note that feathers from different parts of the bird are specialized for different functions.*

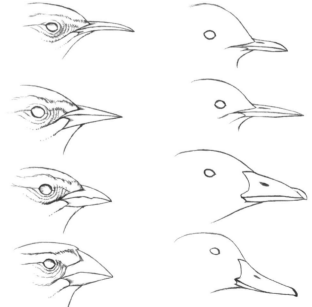

Variation in bill shapes. All species share a fundamentally similar bill structure: the gape, gonys, feathering around the base of the bill, and the bill itself have more in common among different species than not.

The basic feather groups of a
Song Sparrow, *typical of all*
passerines.

scapulars

rump

tail

uppertail coverts

mantle

nape

supercilium

crown

lores

tertials

secondaries

primaries

vent

throat

primary coverts

malar

auriculars

flanks

breast

greater coverts

median coverts

tibia

sides

alula

bend of wing

belly

tarsus

auriculars

nape

mantle

scapulars

malar

throat

breast

auriculars

malar

throat

nape

mantle

scapulars

breast

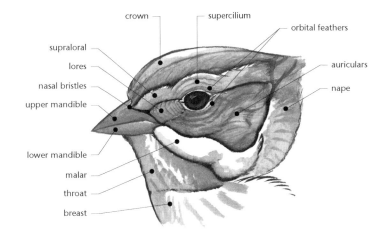

crown

supercilium

orbital feathers

supraloral

lores

auriculars

nasal bristles

nape

upper mandible

lower mandible

malar

throat

breast

69

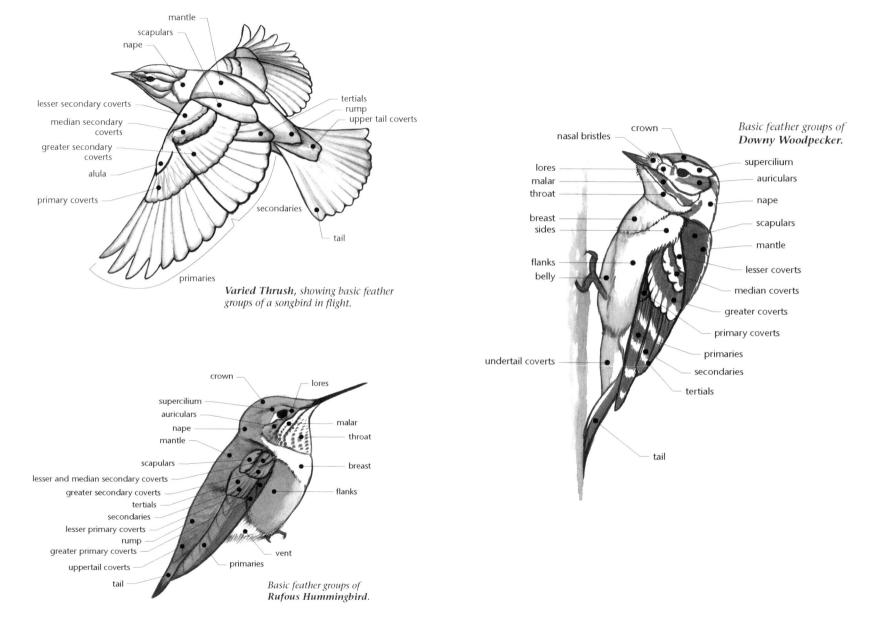

mantle
scapulars
nape
lesser secondary coverts
median secondary coverts
greater secondary coverts
alula
primary coverts
primaries
tertials
rump
upper tail coverts
secondaries
tail

Varied Thrush, *showing basic feather groups of a songbird in flight.*

crown
nasal bristles
lores
malar
throat
breast
sides
flanks
belly
undertail coverts
supercilium
auriculars
nape
scapulars
mantle
lesser coverts
median coverts
greater coverts
primary coverts
primaries
secondaries
tertials
tail

Basic feather groups of **Downy Woodpecker.**

crown
supercilium
auriculars
nape
mantle
scapulars
lesser and median secondary coverts
greater secondary coverts
tertials
secondaries
lesser primary coverts
rump
greater primary coverts
uppertail coverts
tail
lores
malar
throat
breast
flanks
vent
primaries

Basic feather groups of **Rufous Hummingbird.**

70

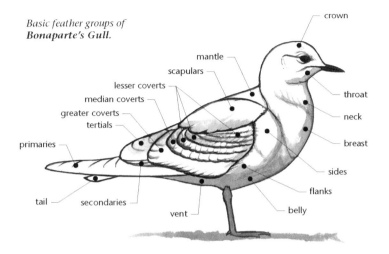

Basic feather groups of
Bonaparte's Gull.

- crown
- mantle
- scapulars
- lesser coverts
- median coverts
- greater coverts
- tertials
- primaries
- tail
- secondaries
- vent
- throat
- neck
- breast
- sides
- flanks
- belly

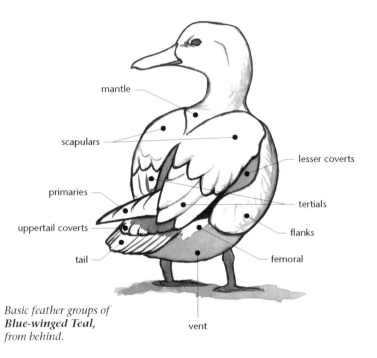

Basic feather groups of
Blue-winged Teal,
from behind.

- mantle
- scapulars
- primaries
- uppertail coverts
- tail
- lesser coverts
- tertials
- flanks
- femoral
- vent

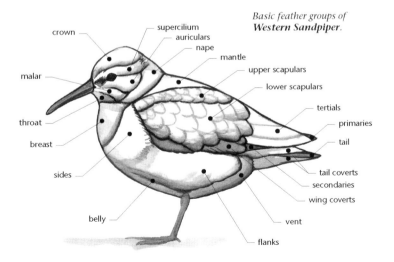

Basic feather groups of
Western Sandpiper.

- crown
- superscilium
- auriculars
- nape
- mantle
- upper scapulars
- lower scapulars
- tertials
- primaries
- tail
- tail coverts
- secondaries
- wing coverts
- vent
- flanks
- malar
- throat
- breast
- sides
- belly

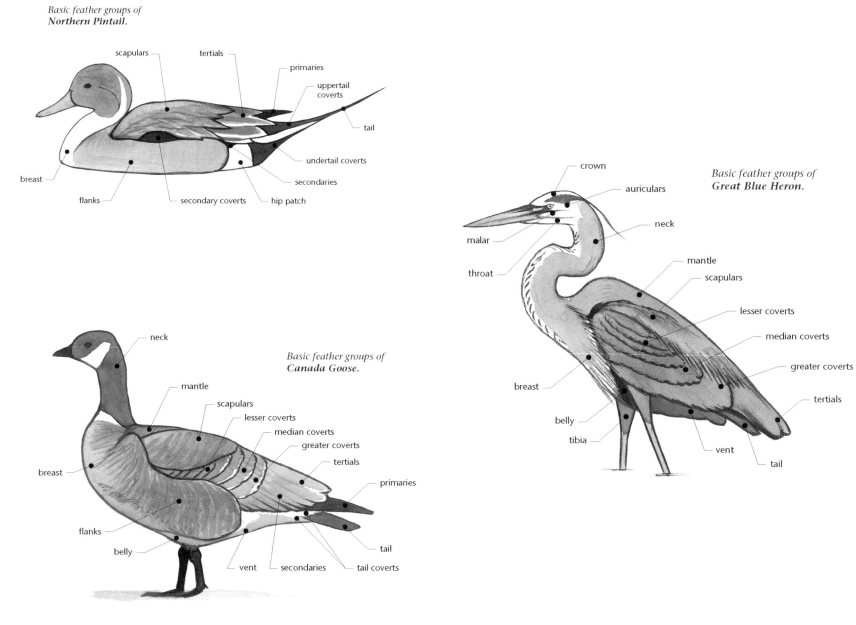

Basic feather groups of
Northern Pintail.

scapulars

tertials

primaries

uppertail
coverts

tail

breast

undertail coverts

flanks

secondaries

secondary coverts

hip patch

Basic feather groups of
Great Blue Heron.

crown

auriculars

neck

malar

throat

mantle

scapulars

lesser coverts

median coverts

greater coverts

breast

tertials

belly

tibia

vent

tail

neck

Basic feather groups of
Canada Goose.

mantle

scapulars

lesser coverts

median coverts

greater coverts

tertials

primaries

breast

flanks

belly

vent

secondaries

tail coverts

tail

72

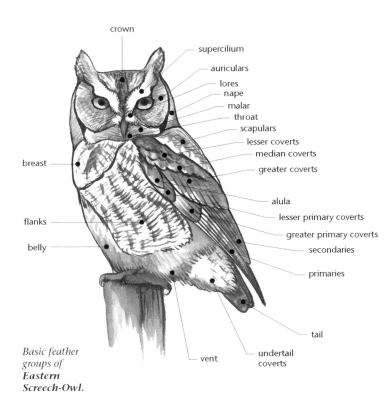

crown

supercilium

auriculars

lores

nape

malar

throat

scapulars

lesser coverts

median coverts

greater coverts

alula

lesser primary coverts

greater primary coverts

secondaries

primaries

breast

flanks

belly

tail

vent

undertail coverts

Basic feather groups of **Eastern Screech-Owl.**

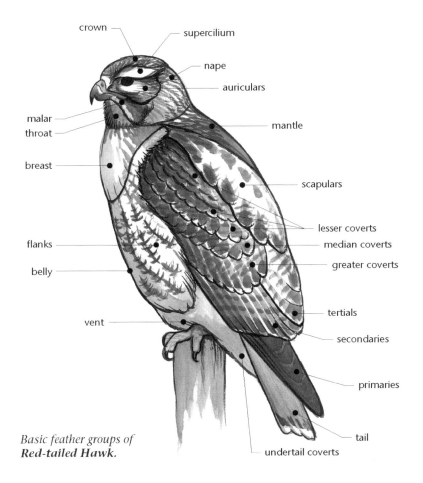

crown

supercilium

nape

auriculars

malar

throat

mantle

breast

scapulars

lesser coverts

flanks

belly

median coverts

greater coverts

vent

tertials

secondaries

primaries

tail

undertail coverts

Basic feather groups of **Red-tailed Hawk.**

A Note About the Authors

DAVID ALLEN SIBLEY is the author and illustrator of the series of successful guides to nature that bear his name, including *The Sibley Guide to Birds*. He has contributed to *Smithsonian, Science, The Wilson Journal of Ornithology, Birding, Birdwatching,* and *North American Birds,* and to *The New York Times*. He is the recipient of the Roger Tory Peterson Award for Lifetime Achievement from the American Birding Association and the Linnaean Society of New York's Eisenmann Medal.

CECILIA LEHAR, a fashion illustrator, most recently drew the line art for *Vogue Colors A to Z*. Lehar worked at *Vogue Patterns* and created period costume illustrations for the Philadelphia Museum of Art. She and her husband are avid birders.

A Note on the Type

ITC Barcelona was designed in 1981 by Ed Benguiat (b. 1927), an American type designer and calligrapher who created many popular midcentury fonts, including Souvenir and Tiffany.

Barcelona is a serif typeface with almost decorative details. The bold and heavy weights include some unique twists to a number of characters and numerals that are slightly rounder than those of the other weights.

Printed and bound by RR Donnelley, Inc., Reynosa, Mexico

Designed and composed by Cassandra Pappas